Host

ERIC PRUM & JOSH WILLIAMS

—— WITH ——

LAUREN SLOSS

PHOTOGRAPHY BY SCOTT BLEICHER

D

DOVETAIL

CONTENTS

DRINK

FEED YOUR FRIENDS

One of our biggest passions has always been bringing friends together over homemade meals and drinks. What started as a habit of throwing raucous dinner parties as roommates in college has evolved into hosting (slightly) more refined get-togethers in and around New York City. We recently realized that we've cooked and drunk our way through much of our time in the city—preparing casual meals for our (future) wives in our tiny apartment kitchens, celebrating birthdays with barbecue blowouts on local rooftops, hosting hours-long post-surf dinners on weekends away at the beach—and we've loved every minute of it. For us, cooking for friends has been key to maintaining sanity amid the craziness of urban living. And in an era in which coming together over a meal is rare, it has become more valuable than ever.

We're lucky: Our educations and career paths have introduced us to eating and drinking cultures across the United States and around the world. After working in restaurant kitchens and attending professional culinary school in Italy, we started a catering company together back at college. Today we channel our culinary passions through our Brooklyn-based food-and-beverage design company, W&P Design. We're as enthusiastic about creating new ideas in food and drink as we are about sharing those ideas and experiences with others, whether through late-night meals for friends or via our company's products. But the best part of our journey over the years has been the chance to connect with a diverse crew of food and drink enthusiasts around the globe—people who, it turns out, also get this same great joy from cooking, eating and drinking with their friends. From San Francisco to Austin and Stockholm to Hong Kong and beyond, we've encountered young city dwellers hungry for the same thing: to come together and eat, drink and foster community with others.

But how do you achieve this in the modern urban environment? It's not easy. Small apartments present their own cooking challenges (you only need two burners on that stove, right?), and free time seems to be a scarce commodity. Don't forget to factor in the changes in our collective taste buds, which have evolved to expect fresher, more flavorful meals regardless of whether they're served in a restaurant or at home.

With all this in mind, we searched for a guide to how real people cook and entertain today. What we found was a wide gap between the Cooking 101 tomes and restaurant cookbooks that focus on recipes from (and often for) professional kitchens. Most of the basic instructional cookbooks we encountered were dense and outdated, often written from a bygone vantage point that didn't account for today's tastes (or access to ingredients). What once was considered exotic and hard to find is now readily available and, frequently, expected (see "*harissa*" and "cocktail bitters").

The chef- and bartender-driven cookbooks on store shelves, while beautiful and inspiring, often present aspirations that are unattainable given the realities of modern urban living. Their recipes might be modified for today's home cook (e.g., scaled down from gallons to ounces), but ultimately they're rooted in the commercial kitchen, requiring hours of prep time and dominating a small kitchen space—the last thing you want when friends are coming over.

Where was the book offering a clear and honest vision of how today's urbanites could simply eat, drink and entertain better?

Our solution: *Host*. Our techniques, recipes and tips come from our personal experiences over the past decade of cooking, bartending and entertaining in our homes—post-grad shares to "grown-up" apartments alike—and all are driven by three underlying principles:

1. Keep it simple. We have limited time for cooking and not much space in our homes to do it, so we created Host with these constraints in mind. Although our recipes are simple to follow, we haven't dumbed down any techniques or compromised on flavor. Are we promising 12-minute recipes that will spring out of your slow cooker carb-free? Definitely not. What we do offer are unfussy, elegant dishes and drinks that are worth your precious time and a place on your table.

2. Use fewer, better ingredients. How do you keep dishes and cocktails simple? By using fewer and better ingredients. Living in an urban area (like New York) has many advantages, and one of them is access to fantastic ingredients. The more flavor each ingredient brings, the fewer the number of ingredients (and the less time) needed for you to turn out stellar meals and drinks.

3. Make people happy. When it comes to hosting friends, at the end of the day (or night), it's all about making people happy. Cities can be crazy, busy, gritty places; when you bring friends together in your home, you create an oasis from the hectic world around you. Put your guests first, keep things fun and casual and throw in a surprise (or two) whenever you can.

At the beginning of this book, we list (with the above principles in mind) the essential tools and ingredients to have on hand for crafting cocktails and preparing food. We explain how you easily can outfit your kitchen and bar with fewer, better items—from pantry staples to different kinds of bitters—to amplify the flavors in your dishes and drinks, and we give tips for tracking down the best, freshest ingredients in your area.

The recipes in *Host* are split into two sections, covering two equally important topics: food ("Eat") and beverages ("Drink"). The order of recipes in each section is free flowing and matches up with how we think about hosting. "Eat" is organized similarly to how we throw parties; it starts with bites and snacks and builds up to large-format dishes. In the second section, "Drink," the recipes start light and bright and build to darker, boozier sipping cocktails, so you can pick your style of cocktail based on season, occasion and mood. Throughout the book, we also share photos, stories and recipes from some of our favorite gatherings with friends, from a summer feast in Montauk to a Sunday brunch in the dead of a Brooklyn winter.

That's *Host* in a nutshell: an honest, modern guide to eating, drinking and feeding your friends. Our hope is that this book helps and inspires you to cook, mix and host your way to a better life, wherever you call home.

Eric & Josh

We've lived in New York City for nearly 10 years. There's so much to love about this huge, crazy place, including its amazing food and drinks scene. But a surplus of expansive apartments with cupboard-filled kitchens isn't one of New York's strong points—especially when you're fresh out of college and living in a 200-square-foot apartment with 10 roommates (unfortunately only a slight exaggeration). At any rate, we've had almost a decade to figure out how to host all of our friends in this urban environment and its tiny apartments.

It may seem daunting to put on a full-scale dinner party when you have a shoebox-size kitchen in a fifth-floor walk-up, but we've found that small spaces have made our kitchens lean, mean party-hosting machines. Because we've cooked in all manner of small spaces, we've figured out what the absolute essentials are for crafting a memorable, food-and-drink-filled gathering. In this section, we lay out the cooking and cocktail tools and ingredients you should have on hand in your home.

After years of searching our city for the best ingredients we could find, we also have some favorite methods and tips for tracking them down—a kind of urban foraging. Don't worry: this doesn't involve digging through the neighborhood park for miner's lettuce or rare mushrooms. It's more about establishing and maintaining relationships with farmers, finding the best local butchers and fishmongers and tracking down secret-weapon sources for cocktail ingredients.

KITCHEN TOOLS

We all have that friend who has a kitchen gadget for every imaginable task, from slicing avocados to shelling eggs, and even toasting tacos. As fun as an overstocked kitchen might be, all that single-purpose gear is unnecessary, especially when you're short on space.

These are the essential kitchen tools that we use on a regular basis. Even as we've upgraded to larger apartments and kitchens over the years, we still prefer to keep our arsenal of cooking tools small, with an emphasis on fewer, better products. You can always have more, but these are our absolute must-haves. These, and our 3D–pancake–printing robot, of course.

SMALL SKILLET

6 – 8 inches in diameter

We use our small stainless steel skillet for cooking single-serving items and small amounts of ingredients for multipart dishes or for reheating portions of leftovers. Cooking in a regular pan (versus nonstick) helps to develop a better crust and caramelization.

LARGE SKILLET

10 – 12 inches in diameter

Same story, larger pan. Our large stainless steel skillet has the same crust-caramelization bonuses but is great for larger batches of ingredients. The larger surface area also allows you to avoid crowding the pan when searing meat and seafood.

LARGE NONSTICK SKILLET

10 – 12 inches in diameter

We use a large nonstick skillet for eggs, seafood and other ingredients prone to sticking. You won't develop the same flavorful bits (called the fond) on the bottom of your pan as you do with stainless steel, but a nonstick pan lets you cook trickier ingredients with ease.

SMALL SAUCEPAN

2-quart capacity

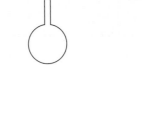

We use a small saucepan for preparing smaller amounts of sauces and syrups; boiling or poaching eggs; and melting butter over low heat (for melting, we prefer using the stovetop to the microwave whenever possible).

LARGE STOCK POT

6-quart capacity or greater

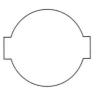

A large stock pot takes up a lot of real estate but has a wide variety of uses. We use ours for preparing large quantities of sauces and syrups and for blanching vegetables and boiling pasta. It also doubles as an extra-large mixing bowl when mixing cocktails ahead of time.

ENAMELED CAST-IRON DUTCH OVEN

6-quart capacity or greater

We're a little obsessed with our enamel-coated cast-iron Dutch oven. The pot's cast-iron core holds enough steady heat to sear meat before a slow cook or braise (a huge win for flavor and texture). And it holds heat evenly when you move everything to the oven, allowing for consistent cooking and temperature all around.

BAR TOOLS

There has been an explosion of varieties of bar tools on the market lately as making cocktails at home has become more popular (two very enthusiastic thumbs up for that!). We love a well-stocked home bar, and these tools are the key pieces you need to start shaking and stirring up drinks at your place. With these you can make just about any cocktail recipe; from here you can expand your collection if you want to take your drink making to the next level.

SHAKER

There are several types of cocktail shakers, but we prefer a three-piece cobbler shaker—for ease of use and for how great it looks on your home bar. Its three parts are: a shaker base, a strainer and a cap. To use it, simply add your ingredients, put the strainer and cap on and shake up your cocktail. You'll want a shaker with capacity of about 30 ounces, for shaking multiple drinks at once.

MIXING GLASS

Having a high-quality mixing glass on your home bar is just as important as having a shaker; both are used frequently but for different types of cocktails. We recommend a mixing glass that can hold at least 20 ounces for stirring multiple cocktails in one batch. Seek out a heavy-bottomed, tempered-glass build with a tapered spout, to give you maximum stability and pouring ease. If you ever find yourself without a mixing glass, a standard pint glass works well in a pinch.

CARAFE OR PITCHER

Making large batches of cocktails is helpful when you're entertaining a crowd, and a good carafe is a must for large-format drinks. We suggest an extra-large capacity of at least 32 ounces for this purpose. Be sure to find a carafe that has a thick base to allow you to muddle ingredients.

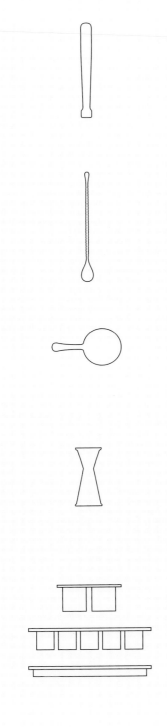

MUDDLER

A muddler is used to crush ingredients (everything from fruit to fresh herbs) to release and build flavors in cocktails. We suggest a classic wooden muddler, which is safe to use with glass and metal cocktail shakers and heavy mixing glasses. (Make sure it's at least 8 inches long, so that it will reach the ingredients.) The end of your muddler should be flat; any sharp teeth will tend to shred your ingredients, and you'll end up chewing your cocktail.

BAR SPOON

A bar spoon is a multipurpose tool that can be used to stir cocktails and measure small amounts of potent cocktail ingredients. It also doubles as an ice cracker if needed (prepare for an ice shower though!). We suggest a long spoon with a weighted handle and a spiral construction if possible, which helps in the stirring process.

STRAINER

To strain your finished stirred cocktails, you need a basic strainer. We recommend a julep strainer for versatility; its larger holes and simple construction make it easy to use and clean.

JIGGER

Used to measure liquid ingredients for cocktails, a jigger is a must for home bars. We suggest picking up a double-sided stainless steel jigger with a 1:2 measurement (e.g., one end of the jigger measures ¾ ounce, the other 1½ ounces). If you need to measure out an amount that's different from your jigger size, just use the side that matches closest and estimate the amount by eye (this is not rocket science!).

ICE TRAYS

We suggest having the trays to make three main types of ice: 2-to 3-inch large cubes, 1-inch square cubes and crushed ice. With these options, you can make any type of cocktail. There are a wide variety of ice trays out there, but we suggest tracking down flexible silicone trays for maximum ease of use and durability.

SERVING TOOLS

Someday when we have big kitchens, we'll have dedicated serving platters and bowls for every single dish we could possibly make. For now, though, rather than construct elaborate leaning towers of platters on top of our refrigerators, we prefer to limit our collection to a handful of good-quality serving pieces that can be used for more than one purpose (e.g., a cutting board that also works as a serving tray).

BOARDS, SMALL

12 inches long

Small wooden boards can be used for food prep as well as for serving appetizers such as meat and cheese, olives and toasts. Use a board that has two functional sides, so you can use one side for prep, quickly wash and dry it, and flip it over for serving.

BOARDS, LARGE

18 inches long

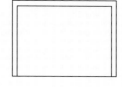

Large wooden boards can be used to serve large-format main dishes like big cuts of meat, whole roasted chickens and grilled fish. We suggest a wooden board that's flat on one side, for food prep, and sloped on the other, for carving and serving (also known as a "trencher"). The sloped side has a well that makes for much easier cleanup; better yet, it allows you to save those meat juices for sauces or for pouring over finished dishes.

BOWLS

Small (6 inches wide), medium (10 inches), large (14 inches)

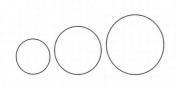

Bowls can be used both for basic food prep and for serving dishes like pastas, salads and vegetable sides. Durable ceramic or stoneware bowls create a solid base for tossing salads and pastas while also looking great on the table.

FARMERS' MARKETS

If we had to pick a favorite place to shop for ingredients, our local farmers' market would win, every time. It's an incredible resource that, if you're lucky, is within walking distance of your home. In addition to being the best place to find fresh, in-season produce (for both cooking and mixing cocktails), it's also a reliably excellent spot to find local cheeses, honey, meats and other prepared foods.

It's good to have a plan when heading to the market, particularly in high season, when stalls are bursting with great-looking produce. We use these strategies when hitting up our market, and they haven't failed us yet.

GO EARLY

Yeah, we get that sleeping in might be your number-one weekend priority, but getting to the market early in the morning means that you're going to get the very best of what these vendors have to offer. And you may run into chefs from some of your favorite restaurants, because they're showing up early too. The best produce is going to go first, and fast, which is reason enough to be in on the action as early as possible. Practically speaking, if you're planning for a party later that day, an early morning start gives you plenty of time to hustle to a grocery store to scoop up any other ingredients you need.

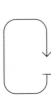

WALK BEFORE YOU BUY

Walk the entire length of the market, at least once, before buying anything. It's easy to get caught up in those really incredible looking tomatoes at the first stall, but there may be even better (and less expensive!) tomatoes a few stalls down. At any rate, you'll get a better idea of what is available, and of the best places to buy certain things. We also find ourselves getting inspired by ingredients we see during our preview round, which leads to new dish ideas or tweaks to existing ones.

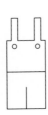

ASK THE FARMER

This is a big one: talk to your farmers! We love getting to know the people selling our produce. They will always have the best handle on what ingredients are at peak ripeness on any given day, and they can tell you what to expect in the coming weeks. We've also received some insightful cooking tips from farmers—anyone with that much knowledge about a specific fruit or vegetable has great ideas about how to prepare it.

SEAFOOD AND BUTCHER SHOPS

We're huge fans of specialized seafood and butcher shops. It's an old-school model that we're glad to see making a comeback: small storefronts focusing on one kind of food or service, and doing it really well (versus the supermarket, where everything's in one place and, too frequently, mass produced). Indie fishmongers and butchers are making a point to source the very best quality fish and meat (from sustainability-minded fishermen and fish farms and animal-friendly farms and ranches), and they're doing so in seasonal ways.

Right, seasonal. Different kinds of fish and meat peak at certain times of year, just like fruits and vegetables. Getting to know your fishmonger and butcher is a great way to find out what proteins are best on any given day. The products at these shops may be a little pricier than those at your average grocery counter, but we feel good knowing that we're using fish that's environmentally sustainable and "happy meat." We also like forming relationships with experts; your fishmonger and butcher can help you out with a few key items that will make your prep and cooking much easier.

CLEANING / BUTCHERING
Do you need that arctic char scaled and filleted or that whole chicken cut into quarters? Your fishmonger or butcher can help you out with that. Not only does that save you time, it avoids the inevitable fish scale explosion or chicken juice spillage once you're back home.

COOKING ADVICE
Speaking with the friendly folks behind the fish or meat counter can yield some choice cooking tips. Your fishmonger or butcher is guaranteed to have opinions on preferred cooking methods, as well as lesser-known species and cuts you could try— an opportunity to expand your food horizons.

SPECIAL ORDERS
Looking to cook a big whole fish or throw a pig roast in your backyard? These are the guys to call in advance, as they can place custom orders with local distributors, fishermen and farmers, and hook you up with the goods you need.

JUICE BARS

Fresh juice is a huge win for cocktails. It adds a ton of flavor that you can't find in the prepackaged stuff. That's why most fancy cocktail bars use hardcore professional juicers. But these juicers are expensive and take up valuable counter space. So we're going to let you in on a cocktail-making secret: juice bars.

The same place you buy your five-day cleanses and kale–beet–ginger–pineapple juice (which is delicious) will also sell you single-ingredient fresh juices, especially if you call ahead. This is a clutch move when you're planning large batches of cocktails, saving you huge amounts of time and headaches. Call a few days in advance for large orders to avoid any confused looks when you ask for a half-gallon of cucumber juice.

The following juices are our go-to orders ahead of throwing a party where we will be serving fresh juice-based cocktails, and are stocked by the majority of neighborhood juice bars.

GINGER JUICE
Fresh ginger adds a kick of heat to cocktails that can't be recreated with bottled ginger soda or syrups. The go-to move: buy fresh ginger juice in small quantities (a little bit goes a long way) and mix up your own fresh ginger beer.

CITRUS JUICE
Squeezing 32 limes for a DIY margarita bar or a sack of grapefruits for a brunch cocktail can be a serious time suck. Most local juice bars carry a wide variety of citrus (lemons, limes, oranges, grapefruit) and can juice them to order in bulk.

PINEAPPLE JUICE
Canned pineapple juice can't match up with the fresh stuff. Planning to make piña coladas for a crowd? Stock up on fresh pineapple juice from your neighborhood juice bar.

CUCUMBER JUICE
Cucumber juice can add a verdant green hue and savory note to G&T's and other cocktails. Try to pick this juice up the same day as you will be using it as the color fades quickly after juicing.

LOCAL MAKERS AND SPECIALTY STORES

"Locally sourced" has become a clichéd descriptor on menus and in stores. But never let it discourage you from seeking out the thoughtful, ingredient-driven products that local makers in your area are creating. There's been a boom of food and drink start-ups over the past few years, and we're delighted to see everything from cheese-makers to whiskey distilleries popping up in our Brooklyn neighborhood. In addition to supporting our fellow entrepreneurs, we've found that these locally made products are usually really, really good and give everything we cook a sense of place.

We also like to look beyond our neighborhood and borough for great products. New York is a massive, gloriously diverse city, and we try to take advantage of that as often as possible. You'll notice recipes in this book that feature Middle Eastern, Mexican, Korean and Vietnamese ingredients. There are dedicated markets in neighborhoods all over most cities—often set up to serve local communities—and they are an incredible resource for new ingredients and cooking inspiration. Talk to the men and women running these shops, and ask for advice about ingredients and maybe even their favorite things to cook at home.

Springtime in Brooklyn feels like magic. After months of cold temperatures and gray skies, the air suddenly feels softer, warmer. And those first warm days beg for a serious celebration. We like to honor the first spring weekend and usher in the season by getting friends together for an evening backyard barbecue, sitting outside and soaking in the fresh air for as long as possible.

Because it's our first chance to use the grill in months (or at least our first chance without wearing a parka), we organize the menu around live-fire cooking. Everything from a grilled squid starter to caveman-size steaks gets at least a kiss of smoke from the fire. We start things off by raising a glass to the season—a glass filled with a refreshing, spring-friendly cucumber and gin cocktail.

THE BACK-GARDEN COCKTAIL

A toast to spring demands a fresh, blooming cocktail—and that's just what the Back Garden is. We quickly infuse gin with cucumber and mint in a blender, giving the drink a verdant hue. You can prepare this ahead of time (just add the ice when you're ready to serve), which leaves you more time to focus on the grill and your guests. We love this drink with a dry, herbaceous gin, but vodka works well too.

MAKES 10 TO 12 COCKTAILS

32 ounces fresh cucumber juice

16 ounces fresh lime juice

16 ounces simple syrup

10 mint sprigs, plus 10 sprigs for garnish

16 ounces gin

10 cucumber wheels

10 lime wheels

In a blender, combine the cucumber juice, lime juice, simple syrup and 10 mint sprigs. Blend at low speed until the mint is finely chopped, about 10 seconds. Using a fine-mesh strainer, strain the mixture into a large serving vessel. Add the gin and ice to fill and garnish with the remaining mint sprigs, cucumber wheels and lime wheels. Serve immediately, pouring the cocktail over ice in individual glasses.

GRILLED SQUID LETTUCE WRAPS WITH NUOC CHAM

This family-style appetizer was inspired by some of our favorite Vietnamese dishes, in which seafood is served alongside a plate of big-leaf lettuce and herbs. The balance of hot and cold, cooked and raw, is as dynamic as it is delicious. Here we like to preserve squid's fresh flavor and snappiness by flash-searing it over super-high heat on the grill. Guests then tuck the squid and herbs in lettuce leaves and dunk the wraps in *nuoc cham*—a funky Vietnamese dipping sauce that adds a punch of spicy-sweet-sour flavor to each bite.

MAKES 6 SERVINGS

FOR THE NUOC CHAM

1 tablespoon fish sauce

4 tablespoons fresh lime juice

3 tablespoons raw sugar

2 Thai chiles (also known as bird's-eye chiles), thinly sliced

FOR THE SQUID

1 pound whole fresh squid, cleaned

1 tablespoon canola oil

Salt and freshly ground black pepper

12 butterhead lettuce leaves, separated and washed

10 mint sprigs

10 cilantro sprigs

MAKE THE NUOC CHAM

In a small serving bowl, combine the fish sauce, lime juice, sugar and sliced chiles. Stir until the sugar is mostly dissolved. Chill in the refrigerator until ready to serve.

MAKE THE SQUID

Prepare a grill for high heat, placing a cast-iron griddle on the hottest area of the grill (if you don't have a griddle, you can cook the squid directly on the grates). Toss the squid with the oil and season with salt and black pepper. When the grill is very hot, place the squid on the griddle and grill for 30 seconds. Flip the squid and grill it for 30 seconds longer. Transfer to a serving platter or cutting board, cut into 1-inch pieces and serve immediately with the lettuce leaves, mint, cilantro and *nuoc cham*.

CRISPY SPRING POTATOES

MAKES 6 SERVINGS

Salt

2 pounds baby potatoes

6 tablespoons unsalted butter, melted

½ cup olive oil

10 thyme sprigs

4 garlic cloves, unpeeled

Flaky sea salt and freshly ground black pepper

¼ cup finely chopped chives and chive blossoms (if available)

Bring a large pot of water to a boil. Season the water with salt until it tastes like seawater. Add the potatoes and simmer until they're just tender when pierced with a knife, about 20 minutes. Drain and reserve. Heat a cast-iron griddle or two large skillets on the grill or stovetop over medium-high heat. In a small bowl, combine the butter and olive oil. Add a thin layer of the butter-oil mixture to the griddle. On a flat surface, crush each potato slightly with your hands until it just bursts, and then place it on the griddle along with the thyme and garlic. Working in batches, cook the potatoes until crisp and browned on one side, about 4 minutes, then flip and cook until the other side is browned and crisp, about 4 minutes longer. Transfer the potatoes, thyme and garlic to a platter and season with sea salt and pepper. Garnish with the chives and serve immediately.

TOMAHAWK RIB-EYE STEAKS WITH CHARRED-RAMP CHIMICHURRI

Ramps, a type of wild onion, are the first sign at New York's farmers' markets that spring is coming. We like to celebrate the season by pairing a charred-ramp chimichurri with the ultimate backyard barbecue centerpiece: a massive, caveman-size tomahawk rib eye steak (sometimes called an axe-handle rib eye), bone included. In addition to looking badass, one tomahawk can usually feed three to four of your friends (or one really, really hungry one). Because it's so thick, we first sear the steak over high heat to form a crust, then move it to lower, indirect heat to finish it off, ensuring it will be cooked evenly. Spring has never tasted so good.

MAKES 6 SERVINGS

FOR THE CHIMICHURRI

12 ramps, washed and roots trimmed

¾ cup olive oil, plus more for grilling

Flaky sea salt and freshly ground black pepper

2 cups flat-leaf parsley leaves

2 garlic cloves, roughly chopped

2 tablespoons fresh lemon juice

¼ teaspoon red pepper flakes

FOR THE STEAKS

Two 2½-pound tomahawk rib-eye steaks (or thick bone-in rib-eye steaks), about 2½ inches thick

Canola oil

Salt and freshly ground black pepper

MAKE THE CHIMICHURRI

Set up a charcoal grill for indirect grilling: pile coals on one side of the grill and light them, reserving the other side for indirect cooking. In a bowl, toss the ramps with olive oil to coat and season with salt and pepper. Grill over direct high heat, turning frequently until charred, about 5 minutes. Remove the ramps from the grill and let cool. In a blender, combine the grilled ramps, parsley, garlic, lemon juice and red pepper flakes. Blend on medium speed, slowly adding the ¾ cup olive oil in a steady stream. Continue blending for 10 seconds until all the solid ingredients are coarsely chopped. Transfer to a serving dish and set aside.

MAKE THE STEAKS

Rub the steaks with canola oil and season liberally all over with salt and pepper. When the grill is very hot, place the steaks directly over the coals. Grill the steaks until they're charred on one side, about 5 minutes, then flip them and sear the other side, about 5 minutes longer. Move the steaks to the cool side of the grill, cover and cook over indirect heat until a meat thermometer inserted near the bone reaches 130° F (for medium rare), about 10 minutes. Remove the steaks from the grill and let rest, tented under foil, for 10 minutes. Slice parallel to the bone and serve with the chimichurri.

MARKET RADISHES
WITH BUTTER AND SEA SALT

It's hard to believe that something so simple can be so memorable. This classic snack is all about contrasting flavor and texture: the spicy, bracing crispness of radishes; the creamy richness of butter; the satisfying pop of ocean-tinged salt. Because just three ingredients are involved, make sure they're great ones — get the freshest radishes you can find, along with high-quality local butter and flaky sea salt.

MAKES 4 SERVINGS

4 tablespoons unsalted butter, softened

3 tablespoons flaky sea salt

12 radishes, including stems and greens, washed and chilled

On a serving plate or board, spread a thick schmear of butter. Mound the sea salt close to the butter and pile the radishes on the plate or board. Guests will take radishes by the stem, dip them in the butter and sprinkle with sea salt. Serve immediately.

WATERMELON AND JICAMA WITH LIME, CHILE AND SEA SALT

We fell in love with watermelon served with lime and chile in Sayulita, a Mexican surfing village near Puerto Vallarta. After an afternoon surf session, we headed to the main square for well-earned margaritas, only to be distracted by a cart piled high with freshly sliced, brightly colored fruits. Served in plastic cups and doused with lime and chile, this street snack was one of the best post-surf bites we had ever had (seawater up our noses and all). Here, we deconstruct it to create a party-friendly, build-your-own appetizer. Sweet watermelon and refreshing jicama pair wonderfully with lime and smoky Mexican chile powder; sea salt adds a taste of the ocean air. If watermelon is out of season, cucumbers and mangoes are excellent substitutes.

MAKES 4 SERVINGS

½ medium watermelon, chilled and cut into 2- to 3-inch pieces

1 large jicama—chilled, peeled and cut into pieces to match the watermelon

Juice of 2 limes

3 tablespoons Mexican chile powder

3 tablespoons flaky sea salt

On a serving plate or board, arrange the watermelon and jicama pieces. To serve, set out three small bowls: one with the lime juice, one with the chile powder and one with the sea salt. Guests will dip the watermelon and jicama into the lime juice and then into the sea salt and chile powder.

CHEESE BOARDS

It's pretty much a law: Whenever we get people together, we serve a cheese board. Not only is it a dead-simple appetizer option, it's also a universal favorite—everyone loves cheese, especially the good stuff. Although a good board is simple to execute, the sheer number of options can be overwhelming. What types of cheese (hard or soft, cow or goat, and so on) should you get? What do you want to serve with the cheese? We have six surefire steps you can take to make your cheese board the best it can be.

STEPS TO A GREAT CHEESE BOARD

1. Talk to your cheesemonger. Tell him or her what kind of gathering you're having, and what you think you'd like to serve. They can help you pick the right combination. (And always remember to taste before you buy!)

2. Limit the number of selections. Yes, you want all of the cheeses, but for party purposes, try to limit yourself to three to five choices; any more can be overwhelming for your guests. The other 50 cheeses will be waiting for the next party.

3. Balance the board. Get a mixture of cheese types, considering texture (hard and soft) as well as milk type (cow, goat, sheep or blends).

4. Keep it local. Try to include at least one local offering; it will give you and your guests a taste of your region. Plus, some types of fresh cheese taste better when they haven't traveled long distances to get to your board.

5. Serve at room temperature. Take your cheese out of the fridge and let it sit unwrapped for about an hour before serving, to let it breathe and come to room temperature. Losing the chill will result in fuller-flavored bites.

6. Cut first. Preslicing cheese before your guests get to it saves you from having a hot mess of a cheese board later. It makes things easier for guests too. Cut your cheeses no more than 30 minutes before you plan on serving them; any earlier and they may dry out. Skip this step for runny, super creamy cheeses.

Tomme d' Aydius
raw goat, aydius, france
A great washed rind tomme from the Valle D'Aspe in the Pyrénées. It's a superb aged goat that is both nutty and sweet, but still has an earthy bite. Truly a cheese not to be passed bye. Pair with champagne and pate.

du Nord, Mons
ance
a glorious color! See what a little carrot can do. This stunning cheese make you grin from ear to ear; one bite ou'll know, now that tastes like cheese. with an Alsatian ale.

Tomme d'Estaing
thermalized sheep, aveyron, fran
What a treat for all you Fr a sheep's milk cheese that fungal earthiness that it's your mouth open in the c a densely wooded forest September when all the r down upon the slowly d there, it's Goldilocks, an to her…Pair with a savo

RICOTTA TOAST
WITH ANCHOVIES AND SHALLOTS

This toast will convert even the biggest anchovy skeptics. Instead of the fishiness that the anti-anchovy camp expects (and dislikes), anchovies are more about umami and salt; there's a little funk there, but in the right dish it gets balanced by richer, mellow-flavored ingredients. In this recipe, we use the little fish almost like a seasoning, adding a briny, savory spike to rich, creamy ricotta.

MAKES 4 SERVINGS

8 slices rustic bread (about ¼ inch thick)

¾ cup whole-milk ricotta

6 anchovy fillets (preferably salt packed)

1 medium shallot, finely chopped

1 teaspoon olive oil

Flaky sea salt and freshly ground
black pepper

In a toaster, skillet or oven, toast the bread until crisp. Transfer to a serving plate or board. Spoon the ricotta onto the toasts, distributing it evenly. Slice each anchovy fillet into thirds lengthwise and place two anchovy slivers on each piece of toast. Top the toast with a bit of shallot, a drizzle of olive oil and a pinch each of salt and pepper, and serve.

WILD MUSHROOM TOAST
WITH CREAM AND THYME

Earthy wild mushrooms take on a wonderful richness after a quick sauté in butter and cream. No exaggeration—once you taste this toast, you might feel the urge to whip up a batch or two of the topping for a quick weeknight pasta dinner. You can find wild mushrooms at most grocery stores, but the best ones will come from the dedicated mushroom guys (or gals) at your local farmers' market. Ask them what they're particularly excited about.

MAKES 4 SERVINGS

8 slices baguette (about ¼ inch thick)

3 tablespoons unsalted butter

2 shallots, finely chopped

3 cups finely chopped mixed wild mushrooms

½ cup half-and-half

1 tablespoon finely chopped thyme leaves

Flaky sea salt and freshly ground black pepper

1 tablespoon finely chopped chives

In a toaster, oven or skillet, toast the baguette slices until crisp.

Meanwhile, in a skillet, melt the butter over medium-high heat. Add the shallots and cook until soft, about 2 minutes. Add the mushrooms and cook, stirring frequently, until the mushrooms are soft, about 3 minutes. Add the half-and-half and the thyme and bring to a simmer. Cook until the liquid has reduced by half, about 3 minutes. Season with salt and pepper to taste. Spoon the mushroom mixture over the toasts and garnish with the chives. Transfer to a serving plate or board and serve immediately.

BUTTERHEAD LETTUCE WITH AVOCADO, RADISH AND PECORINO ROMANO

This versatile salad is one of our all-time favorites. Simple and refreshing, it pairs well with just about any other large dish to round out a great meal. The process of creating the dressing, which contains olive oil, Champagne vinegar and fresh lemon juice, is key; be sure to add the oil first, as it protects the lettuce leaves from the wilt-inducing acidity of the vinegar and citrus.

MAKES 4 SERVINGS

1 head butterhead lettuce,
leaves separated

1 avocado—halved, pitted and thinly
sliced lengthwise

3 radishes, thinly sliced

¼ cup olive oil

1 tablespoon fresh lemon juice

1 teaspoon Champagne vinegar

Flaky sea salt and freshly ground
black pepper

½ cup shaved Pecorino Romano cheese

In a serving bowl, add the lettuce and top with the avocado and radish slices. Drizzle the olive oil over the salad, then add the lemon juice and vinegar. Toss to coat the lettuce with the dressing. Season to taste with salt and pepper. Top with the cheese shavings and serve.

FARMERS' MARKET GREEK SALAD

Greek salads have a bad rep. Considering that many of them are made with wilting lettuce and sad, pink tomatoes, it's no surprise. We hope this recipe will change your mind about Greek salads; it certainly changed ours. We use whatever looks good at the farmers' market to make this salad: in summer that absolutely involves sweet tomatoes and crisp cucumbers, whereas in winter and fall, we swap in roasted root vegetables and kale. We skip the lettuce, too, using a ton of fresh herbs instead, which results in a fresh, hugely flavorful salad.

MAKES 4 SERVINGS

FOR THE VINAIGRETTE

1 tablespoon red wine vinegar

1 tablespoon fresh lemon juice

½ teaspoon fine sea salt

⅛ teaspoon freshly ground black pepper

½ teaspoon dried oregano

¼ cup olive oil

¼ cup canola oil

FOR THE SALAD

2 tomatoes, cut into wedges

1 medium cucumber, cut into
½-inch cubes

1 medium red onion, cut into
½-inch pieces

¼ cup flat-leaf parsley leaves

¼ cup sliced chives (1-inch lengths)

¼ cup roughly torn dill pieces (about
1 inch long)

¼ cup mint leaves

TO FINISH

6 ounces feta cheese, crumbled

1 tablespoon capers (preferably
salt packed)

MAKE THE VINAIGRETTE
In a bowl, whisk together the vinegar, lemon juice, sea salt, pepper and oregano until the salt has dissolved. Add the oils in a slow, steady stream while constantly whisking. Set aside.

MAKE THE SALAD
In a serving bowl, combine the tomatoes, cucumber, red onion and herbs. Add the vinaigrette and toss to combine. Top the salad with the feta and capers and serve.

SPICY MUSTARD GREENS WITH ROASTED CARROTS AND BUTTERMILK DRESSING

This recipe is one of our go-to salads, combining peppery mustard greens with caramelized roasted carrots and a tangy buttermilk dressing. Not only does roasting the carrots add tremendous flavor to this salad, it also can be done well ahead of time, so this dish can come together in a flash when it's time to eat.

MAKES 4 SERVINGS

FOR THE CARROTS

12 small carrots, greens removed

2 tablespoons olive oil

1 pinch flaky sea salt

1 pinch freshly ground black pepper

4 thyme sprigs

FOR THE DRESSING

½ cup buttermilk

½ cup crème fraîche

1 garlic clove, finely chopped

1 teaspoon Champagne vinegar

1 teaspoon fresh lemon juice

1 tablespoon finely chopped chives

¾ teaspoon fine sea salt, plus more for seasoning

⅛ teaspoon freshly ground black pepper, plus more for seasoning

4 cups mustard greens, washed with stems removed

MAKE THE CARROTS

Preheat the oven to 425° F. In a medium bowl, toss the carrots with the olive oil, sea salt and pepper. On a rimmed baking sheet, spread the carrots in a single layer. Scatter the thyme sprigs over the carrots and roast 20 minutes, or until the carrots are caramelized and tender. Let cool.

MAKE THE DRESSING

In a mixing bowl, whisk together the buttermilk, crème fraîche, garlic, Champagne vinegar, lemon juice, chives, sea salt and pepper until combined.

MAKE THE SALAD

In a large serving bowl, toss together the mustard greens and roasted carrots. Top with the buttermilk dressing, toss to combine and season with salt and pepper. Serve immediately.

KALE CAESAR
WITH TOASTED BREADCRUMBS

We can't walk half a block in Brooklyn without tripping over a kale Caesar salad. OK, not quite—but this salad is everywhere, and we're fine with it. Why? Because kale Caesar, done right, is a great salad. With hearty greens and rich, garlicky dressing, it's satisfying, savory and actually healthy. We like to use dark green lacinato, or Tuscan kale, which is more tender and lends itself well to being sliced into thin strips. Breadcrumbs and a ton of sharp Pecorino Romano cheese keep this from being *too* healthy (or at least tasting like it).

MAKES 4 SERVINGS

FOR THE BREADCRUMBS

2 tablespoons olive oil

2 slices country bread, roughly torn into chunks

Salt and freshly ground black pepper

FOR THE DRESSING

½ garlic clove, finely chopped

½ cup finely grated Pecorino Romano cheese

6 tablespoons olive oil

2 tablespoons fresh lemon juice

Fine sea salt and freshly ground black pepper

FOR THE SALAD

1 large bunch lacinato kale (also known as Tuscan, dinosaur or black kale)

¼ cup finely grated Pecorino Romano cheese

MAKE THE BREADCRUMBS

In a skillet, heat the olive oil over medium heat. Add the bread pieces and toast until crispy and golden brown, about 2 minutes. Transfer to a paper towel–lined plate and season with salt and pepper. In a blender or food processor, pulse the toasted bread until pea-size crumbs form (about 15 seconds). Transfer to a bowl and set aside.

MAKE THE DRESSING

In a bowl, whisk together the garlic, ½ cup pecorino cheese, olive oil and lemon juice. Season to taste with salt and pepper.

MAKE THE SALAD

Remove the stems and ribs from the kale and slice the leaves crosswise into ¼-inch ribbons. In a serving bowl, toss the greens with all of the dressing and, using your hands, massage the kale for 30 seconds to help tenderize it. Let the kale rest for 5 minutes. Add the breadcrumbs and toss. Top with the remaining ¼ cup of pecorino cheese and serve.

FRIED OYSTERS
WITH KEWPIE TARTAR SAUCE

In summer, we love to get to the beach for surf and sun as much as possible. Whether we're heading to Montauk for the weekend or escaping to Rockaway Beach for a quick afternoon session, one highlight is the trip there: we can't seem to keep ourselves from stopping at a roadside seafood shack for a to-go container of fried oysters. Briny and crunchy from a buttermilk batter, these oysters bring us back to the beach with the first bite. We make a tartar sauce for dipping using Kewpie mayo, a Japanese mayonnaise made with rice vinegar that's store-bought which to us tastes exactly like a summer day at the beach.

MAKES 4 SERVINGS

FOR THE TARTAR SAUCE

1 cup Kewpie mayonnaise

2 teaspoons sweet relish

3 tablespoon finely chopped red onion

1 tablespoon lemon juice

1 teaspoon Old Bay seasoning

FOR THE OYSTERS

2 cups yellow cornmeal

2 cups all-purpose flour

1 tablespoon Old Bay seasoning

2 cups buttermilk, shaken well

1 pint of shucked oysters, stored in their own liquid

Vegetable oil, for frying

MAKE THE TARTAR SAUCE

In a bowl, combine the mayonnaise, relish, onion, lemon juice and Old Bay seasoning and stir to combine. Set aside in the refrigerator until ready to serve.

MAKE THE OYSTERS

In a medium bowl, mix the cornmeal, flour and Old Bay seasoning together. Pour the buttermilk into a separate bowl. Drain the oysters and place them in the buttermilk. One at a time, lightly coat each oyster in the cornmeal mixture.

In a large pot, heat 2 inches or more of vegetable oil until it reaches 375° F on a frying thermometer. Working in batches (about 6 to 8 oysters at a time), fry the oysters until they're golden, about 1 to 2 minutes. Using a slotted spoon, transfer them to a paper towel–lined plate. When all of the oysters are fried, transfer them to a serving bowl or platter and serve immediately with the tartar sauce on the side.

YELLOWTAIL AGUACHILE

We thought there was no beating ceviche until we tried *aguachile*—a super spicy, incredibly fresh version of ceviche that comes swimming in a serrano pepper–laced chile water. A full-flavored appetizer to serve with beer or margaritas, it's easily scalable to feed a crowd. The major difference between *aguachile* and ceviche is that *aguachile* is served immediately; the seafood isn't left to marinate and cure in the lime juice like ceviche is. This means you want to use the freshest fish you can find and serve this dish right after making it.

In Mexico, *aguachile* is often made with gray-blue shrimp plucked straight from the ocean. We like to use sushi-grade yellowtail (also known as hamachi), but you can substitute whatever fish is freshest at your local seafood market. Be sure to tell your fishmonger that you'll be eating the fish raw and get his or her recommendation.

MAKES 4 SERVINGS

1 serrano chile, roughly chopped

2 small cucumbers, roughly chopped, plus 5 to 6 thin slices, for serving

6 tablespoons fresh lime juice

Flaky sea salt and freshly ground black pepper

¼ cup finely chopped cilantro leaves

½ pound sushi-grade yellowtail

¼ medium red onion, thinly sliced

Tortilla chips, for serving

In a blender, combine the chile, cucumber and lime juice. Blend on high for 1 minute, or until mixture looks like a finely chopped salsa. Using a fine-mesh strainer set over a small bowl, strain the mixture, pressing to extract all the liquid. Season the strained liquid with salt and pepper to taste and stir in the cilantro; this is your chile water, a.k.a. *aguachile*. Refrigerate until ready to serve.

Cut the yellowtail into very thin, 2-inch slices and arrange the pieces in a single layer on the bottom of a shallow bowl. Scatter the red onion and cucumber slices across the fish, then pour the chile water over it. Top with a pinch of sea salt. Serve immediately with tortilla chips.

THREE PEAS WITH RICOTTA AND CHIVES

This recipe shows off a range of spring produce in one sweet and easy dish. We originally came up with this as a pasta topping but found that it was just as good, if not better, on its own. Sweet green peas join snap peas and pea shoots for a super-quick sauté with shallots and butter, then are dotted with creamy, fresh ricotta. Fresh peas definitely are best here, but you can use high-quality frozen ones in a pinch.

MAKES 4 SERVINGS

2 tablespoons unsalted butter

½ cup minced shallots

3 cups green peas (fresh or frozen and thawed)

2 cups fresh sugar snap peas, trimmed

1 cup pea shoots

1 cup whole-milk ricotta

Finely grated zest of 1 lemon

¼ cup thinly sliced chives

Flaky sea salt and freshly ground black pepper

In a large skillet, melt the butter over medium heat. Add the shallots and cook until translucent, about 1 minute. Add the green peas and sugar snap peas and cook until the snap peas are tender, about 2 minutes. Remove from the heat and add the pea shoots, tossing to combine until the shoots are wilted.

Transfer the pea mixture to a medium serving bowl and top with dollops of the ricotta. Sprinkle the peas and ricotta cheese with the lemon zest, chives, sea salt and pepper. Serve immediately.

BURNT VEGGIES

We've got an important message for you: It's time to start burning your vegetables. Seriously. A little bit of char goes a long way, and it will completely change how you think about vegetables. We're not suggesting that you turn your veggies into charcoal briquettes, but do let the cooking process go longer than you might think it should. Extended roasting, grilling and searing lead to caramelization of the vegetables' natural sugars, and create an unbelievably good range of savory-sweet flavors.

BURNT CARROTS
WITH LEBNEH, HONEY AND SESAME

The carrot is the perfect entry-level vegetable for burning: it becomes super caramelized, which brings out its rich sweetness, and takes on a crispy char like a champ. This recipe also showcases *lebneh*, a thick, strained Middle Eastern yogurt that is slightly salty. With its creamy tang, *lebneh* provides a great contrast to the burnt carrots' smoky sweetness, but we love it as a base for most roasted vegetables. Although you can buy high-quality *lebneh* at specialty stores, it's incredibly easy to make at home.

MAKES 4 SERVINGS

FOR THE LEBNEH

2 cups full-fat Greek yogurt

1 pinch of fine sea salt

FOR THE CARROTS

20 small carrots, tops trimmed
to 1 inch

Olive oil

½ teaspoon dried oregano

Flaky sea salt and freshly ground
black pepper

1 tablespoon raw honey

1 teaspoon sesame seeds, for garnish

MAKE THE LEBNEH

Start making the *lebneh* 24 hours before you intend to serve it. In a bowl, combine the yogurt and salt and stir. Over a large bowl, place a fine-mesh strainer lined with a double layer of cheesecloth. Pour the yogurt and salt mixture into the cheesecloth-lined strainer. Cover the strainer and bowl with plastic wrap and refrigerate for 24 hours.

MAKE THE CARROTS

Preheat the oven to 450° F. In a large bowl, toss the carrots with olive oil to coat, oregano, salt and pepper. On a rimmed baking sheet, spread the carrots in a single layer. Roast until they are slightly burnt, tender and caramelized, about 20 minutes. Resist the urge to stir the carrots until they are fully caramelized on one side, then turn them once. Remove from the oven.

Spread the *lebneh* in a thin layer across the bottom of a serving platter or large, shallow serving bowl and top with the roasted carrots. Drizzle the honey and a little bit of olive oil over the carrots and *lebneh*. Garnish with the sesame seeds and a sprinkle of salt. Serve immediately.

CARAMELIZED BRUSSELS SPROUTS WITH APPLES AND BACON

Brussels sprouts and bacon are a magical combination. Here we sauté them with sweet, tart apple cubes for a hearty, warming dish that tastes like the best parts of fall. We start this dish on the stovetop, quickly caramelizing the Brussels sprouts in a hot skillet, and then finish it in the oven. A splash of cider vinegar lends brightness to the dish without taking away from the deep, rich flavors. Try to buy an extra-thick cut of bacon (about ½-inch thick) from your butcher so you can cut it into large, extra-bacony cubes.

MAKES 4 SERVINGS

1½ pounds Brussels sprouts, trimmed and halved

1 apple (preferably Honeycrisp or Pink Lady), peeled and cut into ½-inch cubes

¼ pound slab bacon, cut into ½-inch cubes

2 tablespoons olive oil

Flaky sea salt and freshly ground black pepper

1 tablespoon cider vinegar

Preheat the oven to 400° F. Heat a large, oven-safe skillet over medium-high heat. In a bowl, toss the Brussels sprouts, apple and bacon with olive oil, salt and pepper. Add a thin layer of oil to the pan; when it shimmers, add the Brussels sprouts mixture, ensuring that most of the sprouts are cut side down in the pan. Cook without moving them until they caramelize, about 4 minutes; the sprouts will be almost charred. Stir the mixture, then place the skillet in the oven. Roast until the Brussels sprouts are tender, 8 to 10 minutes. Transfer to a serving dish or bowl, drizzle with cider vinegar and serve.

ARCTIC CHAR WITH CRISPY LEMONS AND ANCHOVY BUTTER

This fish dish is simple and full of flavor, and it can be prepared in minutes thanks to a quick flash under the broiler. The anchovy butter adds an incredible punch of rich, savory flavor; we use anchovy paste in it, but anchovy fillets will work too (just dice them finely and mix them with the butter). A cooking base of lemons nicely infuses the fish with bright citrus and balances the butter's richness. We love to use arctic char for this recipe—it's similar in color and texture to salmon (they're actually distant cousins) but tends to have a more delicate flavor and, even better, is usually more sustainable. This method of cooking works for all kinds of flaky fish, though, including salmon, trout and cod.

MAKES 4 SERVINGS

4 tablespoons unsalted butter, melted

1 teaspoon anchovy paste

2 garlic cloves, finely chopped

½ teaspoon freshly ground black pepper

Olive oil

6 lemons, thinly sliced

Flaky sea salt

2 arctic char fillets (about 1½ pounds)

1 teaspoon finely chopped chives

Preheat the broiler to high. In a small bowl, combine the melted butter, anchovy paste, garlic and pepper and stir to combine.

Brush a large rimmed baking sheet with olive oil. Layer the lemon slices on the sheet, slightly overlapping, creating a bed for the fish fillets. Lightly drizzle the lemons with olive oil and season with sea salt and pepper. Place each fish fillet on the bed of lemons. Pour the anchovy butter over each fillet, distributing evenly. Broil until the fish is almost cooked through, about 5 minutes (cooking time will vary based on thickness). Transfer the fish fillets along with their lemon beds to a platter. Sprinkle with the chives and serve immediately.

BEST. CHICKEN. EVER.

We love grilled chicken. People don't believe us when we say it, but if we could cook and serve one dish for the rest of time, this would be it. There are three steps to great grilled chicken: sourcing, marinating and garnishing. First, look to buy "free-range" or "pasture-raised" chicken from the farmers' market or grocery store, as birds raised free to roam are the most flavorful. Second, a quick marinade before cooking helps amplify the natural flavors of the chicken and keep the meat juicy during grilling. Lastly, a garnish, whether it's a sauce or, in this case, a fresh herb salad (see opposite), can provide an extra kick of flavor to elevate the finished grilled chicken.

FRESH HERB SALAD

This citrus-and-garlic-spiked fresh herb salad complements flavorful grilled chicken—or just about any grilled meat, come to think of it.

MAKES 4 SERVINGS

2 tablespoons olive oil

2 tablespoons fresh lemon juice

1 garlic clove, very thinly sliced

1 large pinch flaky sea salt

1 pinch freshly ground black pepper

½ cup loosely packed parsley leaves

½ cup loosely packed mint leaves

½ cup torn dill (½-inch pieces)

In a medium bowl, stir together the olive oil, lemon juice, garlic, salt and pepper. Add the herbs and toss to combine. Serve immediately.

GRILLED CHICKEN WITH FRESH HERB SALAD AND CHARRED LEMON

After a quick marinade, naturally flavorful free-range chicken gets grilled and topped with our Fresh Herb Salad. Prepare to have your mind blown by the humble bird.

MAKES 4 SERVINGS

1 tablespoon finely chopped garlic

1 tablespoon finely chopped thyme

Zest of 1 lemon

¼ teaspoon finely chopped fennel seeds

½ teaspoon red chile flakes

½ cup olive oil

1 whole free-range chicken (about 2 pounds), cut into eight pieces (2 breasts, thighs, drumsticks and wings each)

Flaky sea salt and freshly ground black pepper

2 lemons, halved

Fresh Herb Salad (page 111)

In a large bowl, stir together the garlic, thyme, lemon zest, fennel seed, chile flakes and olive oil. Season all sides of the chicken sections with sea salt and pepper and then add the chicken to the marinade, making sure all pieces are covered. Let the chicken marinate in the refrigerator for at least 30 minutes.

Preheat a gas or charcoal grill to medium-high heat. Place the chicken pieces skin side down on the grill and cook uncovered until cooked through—approximately 5 minutes per side for the breasts and wings and 7 minutes for the thighs and drumsticks. Place the lemons cut-side down on the grill and cook until charred.

As the chicken pieces cook through and the lemon halves char, remove them from the grill to a serving board or platter. Let the chicken rest for 5 minutes. Serve with the Fresh Herb Salad and the charred lemon on the side.

CRISPY LAMB RIBS WITH HARISSA YOGURT AND MINT SALSA VERDE

An incredibly flavorful yet underutilized cut, lamb ribs take some time and patience to cook but result in a memorably excellent contrast of flavor and textures. We start by braising the ribs until they're very tender, then quickly finish them under the broiler to add a crisp, caramelized crust. The ribs are phenomenal by themselves, but our favorite way to serve them is with *harissa* yogurt—a simple blend of fiery Middle Eastern chile paste and tangy Greek yogurt—and a garlicky, mint-flecked salsa verde.

MAKES 4 SERVINGS

1 tablespoon olive oil, plus more for brushing

5 pounds lamb ribs, excess fat trimmed

Flaky sea salt and freshly ground black pepper

1 cup roughly chopped onion

1 cup roughly chopped carrot

1 cup roughly chopped celery

4 garlic cloves, halved

One 750-milliliter bottle dry white wine

1 quart chicken stock

1 tablespoon dried oregano

4 rosemary sprigs

12 Castelvetrano olives

Mint leaves, for garnish

Harissa Yogurt (see page 117)

Mint Salsa Verde (see page 117)

Preheat the oven to 275° F. In a large, heavy Dutch oven or pot, heat the olive oil over medium-high heat. Season the lamb ribs with salt and pepper and, working in batches, brown the ribs. Drain all but 3 tablespoons of fat. Add the onion, carrot, celery and garlic and cook until slightly browned, about 10 minutes. Add the wine, chicken stock, oregano and rosemary, turn the heat up to high and bring to a boil. Add the lamb ribs and the olives, making sure they're fully submerged in the braising liquid (add water or more wine if they're not). Cover, return the liquid to a boil and transfer the pot to the oven. Cook the ribs, covered, until they're tender and cooked through, about 3 hours. After 2 hours, be sure to check that the level of liquid is still above the ribs and add water or wine as needed.

Remove the pot from the oven and let the ribs rest in the braising liquid for 1 hour. Remove the ribs and olives from the liquid, pat them dry with a towel and place them on a baking sheet. Preheat the broiler to high. Brush the ribs and olives with olive oil and sprinkle with sea salt and pepper. Broil the ribs and olives until the ribs are browned and crispy on top, about 3 minutes. Transfer to a large serving board or platter and garnish with mint leaves and salsa verde. Serve the lamb ribs with the *harissa* yogurt.

HARISSA YOGURT

MAKES 1 CUP

1 cup full-fat Greek yogurt

1 tablespoon *harissa*

1 garlic clove, finely chopped

1 teaspoon lemon juice

Salt and freshly ground black pepper

In a small serving bowl, stir together the yogurt, *harissa*, garlic and lemon juice. Season to taste with salt and pepper.

MINT SALSA VERDE

A simple blend of fresh herbs, garlic and capers, salsa verde is a punchy, versatile sauce, tangy with lemon and full of flavor. Here we use a combination of parsley, chives and mint, but you can substitute any green herbs you like alongside a base of parsley (dill, oregano and basil all work well). We love this mint version with the lamb ribs and *harissa* yogurt, but it also pairs well with most grilled meats and fish (or even drizzled over eggs and slathered on pieces of toast).

MAKES 1 CUP

½ cup finely chopped flat-leaf parsley

¼ cup finely chopped chives

½ cup finely chopped mint

1 garlic clove, finely chopped

1 tablespoon finely chopped capers

Zest, finely grated, and juice of 1 lemon

¾ cup olive oil

Flaky sea salt and freshly ground black pepper

In a small serving bowl, combine the herbs, garlic and capers. Add the lemon zest and juice and olive oil and stir to combine. Season to taste with salt and pepper. The salsa verde will keep for up to 12 hours, covered, in the refrigerator.

GRILLED FISH TACOS WITH CABBAGE SLAW

Nothing says summer quite like a plate of fish tacos. We emphasize the season's backyard-barbecue vibes by grilling a whole, large fish (big enough to feed 10 hungry friends), which can be flaked right off the bone and into warm, waiting tortillas. Use a meaty white fish that can stand up to grilling, like striped bass; your fishmonger will have other great suggestions on this count. Tangy cabbage slaw, spiked with cumin, adds freshness and crunch.

MAKES 10 SERVINGS

FOR THE SLAW

1 teaspoon ground cumin

½ cup white vinegar

1 tablespoon sugar

1 tablespoon mayonnaise

1 teaspoon fine sea salt

3 cups thinly shredded red cabbage (about ½ a small cabbage)

FOR THE FISH

One 4- to 5-pound whole fish (we like striped bass or other white fish), cleaned and scaled

Olive oil

Flaky sea salt and freshly ground black pepper

Tortillas, salsas and fresh herbs, for serving

MAKE THE SLAW

In a large serving bowl, combine the cumin, vinegar, sugar, mayonnaise and salt. Whisk until the sugar and salt dissolve. Add the shredded cabbage to the bowl and toss until it's coated with the dressing. Cover the bowl with plastic wrap or foil. Let the slaw rest in the refrigerator for at least 30 minutes before serving.

GRILL THE FISH

Prepare a grill for medium heat. Pat the fish dry with paper towels, removing as much moisture as possible. Brush the fish with olive oil and season with salt and pepper on all sides (including the inside). Brush the grill grate with oil to prevent the fish from sticking.

Place the fish on the oiled grates and grill, uncovered, until the fish releases from the grates easily, about 10 minutes. Flip the fish, cover and cook until the flesh is white and flaky, about 10 minutes more. Transfer to a serving platter or board. Serve the fish whole, with the slaw, tortillas, salsas and fresh herbs on the side.

GRILLED HANGER STEAK TACOS WITH GOCHUJANG RADISH SALAD

It's hard to go wrong with *carne asada* (grilled beef) tacos. We like hanger steak for these family-style tacos; in addition to being incredibly flavorful, it's an often overlooked cut of meat and therefore usually more affordable than other cuts. We love serving these tacos with a bright, crunchy radish salad, which get a punch of heat from *gochujang*, a spicy-sweet Korean chile paste. You can find it at most groceries and all Korean markets.

MAKES 10 SERVINGS

FOR THE MARINADE

4 garlic cloves, finely chopped

4 tablespoons canola oil

2 teaspoons ground cumin

2 teaspoons Mexican chile powder

FOR THE STEAK

2 whole hanger steaks, about 1 to 1½ pounds each

Salt and freshly ground black pepper

FOR THE RADISH SALAD

2 tablespoons *gochujang*

2 teaspoons olive oil

1 teaspoon lime juice

1 tablespoon honey

10 radishes, thinly sliced

Flaky sea salt and freshly ground black pepper

Tortillas, salsas and fresh herbs, for serving

MAKE THE MARINADE

In a small bowl, combine the garlic, canola oil, cumin and chile powder and stir. Season all sides of the steaks liberally with salt and pepper. Place the steaks in a nonreactive dish and rub the marinade into the steaks. Cover and refrigerate for at least 1 hour.

GRILL THE STEAKS

Remove the steaks from the refrigerator and let them come to room temperature, about 20 minutes. Light a grill. When the grill is hot, grill the steaks over high heat for about 5 minutes per side, until an instant-read thermometer inserted into the center reads 130° F (for medium-rare). Transfer the steaks to a cutting board and let them rest for 10 minutes. Slice the steaks thinly across the grain and serve with the spicy radish salad, tortillas, salsas and fresh herbs.

MAKE THE RADISH SALAD

While the steak is coming to room temperature, in a medium serving bowl, whisk together the *gochujang*, olive oil, lime juice and honey. Add the radishes and season to taste with salt and pepper. Refrigerate until ready to serve.

summer

GATHERING

THE STORMY DITCH

The Stormy Ditch, our take on the classic summer beach cocktail, the Dark and Stormy, combines fresh ginger juice, lime and bourbon. The ginger juice adds an unbeatable punch of flavor and is one of our not-so-secret cocktail ingredients. It might sound exotic and hard to find, but just swing by your local juice bar to get the good stuff.

MAKES 1 COCKTAIL

1½ ounces bourbon

¾ ounce lime juice

½ ounce fresh ginger juice

1 ounce simple syrup

3 ounces club soda

1 lime wheel, for garnish

In a rocks glass filled with ice, combine the bourbon, lime juice, ginger juice and simple syrup and stir briefly. Top with club soda and garnish with the lime wheel. Serve immediately.

DIVER SCALLOPS WITH CHARRED SWEET CORN, BACON AND SCALLIONS

Montauk is the main fishing town on Long Island, and the local docks offer some of the freshest seafood you'll find on the East Coast, including diver scallops, which are harvested by hand instead of with nets dragged over the ocean floor. Taking center stage in this dish, these scallops are lightly grilled and set atop charred summer-sweet corn with crunchy scallions and a squeeze of lemon. When making this for a crowd, we prepare the corn ahead of time and assemble the components at the last possible moment.

MAKES 4 SERVINGS

FOR THE CORN

6 ears of corn, husks removed

1 tablespoon canola oil

2 teaspoons sea salt

1 teaspoon freshly ground black pepper

½ cup of ¼-inch wide bacon cubes

3 tablespoons butter, unsalted

FOR THE SCALLOPS

20 sea scallops

¼ cup olive oil

Sea salt and freshly ground black pepper

½ lemon

2 medium scallions, thinly sliced at an angle (½ cup), for garnish

MAKE THE CORN

Light a grill. Lightly oil the ears of corn with the canola oil. When the grill is very hot, grill the corn over high heat for 5 minutes, turning to get a light char on all sides. Remove the corn from the grill and let it cool. Cut the kernels off the cobs and reserve.

Place a large sauté pan on the stove over medium heat. Add the bacon and cook until crispy, about 5 minutes. Drain the bacon with a slotted spoon and transfer to a paper towel–lined plate. Reserve 1 tablespoon of the rendered bacon fat and discard the rest (or save for another use).

When you're ready to serve, in a large sauté pan melt the butter with the reserved bacon fat over medium heat. Add the corn, salt and pepper and heat through, stirring frequently, for about 5 minutes. Transfer the corn to a serving platter, spreading the kernels into a thick layer.

MAKE THE SCALLOPS

Light the grill (if it's not still lit from the corn). Dry the scallops thoroughly with paper towels and toss with the olive oil. Season lightly with sea salt and pepper. When the grill is very hot, grill the scallops over high heat until just translucent in the middle, about 3 minutes per side (this will depend on how thick your scallops are). Transfer the scallops to the platter of charred corn. Finish with a squeeze of lemon over the platter and garnish with the scallions. Serve immediately.

PEACH AND BLUEBERRY COBBLER WITH VANILLA ICE CREAM

Peaches and blueberries are two of our favorite summertime fruits, and this recipe is all about letting them shine. It's also one of the easiest baked desserts, with little more than a simple batter as its base. We like to bake and serve this dessert in a cast-iron skillet; it crisps the cobbler's edges perfectly and is great looking too. You can make the cobbler one to two hours ahead of time, but it's even better if you serve it straight out of the oven. Just prep the dry and wet ingredients ahead of time, mix them together at the last minute and pop the cobbler into the oven right before starting dinner.

MAKES 8 SERVINGS

1 stick (½ cup) unsalted butter

1 cup all-purpose flour

1 cup sugar

1 tablespoon baking powder

1 cup whole milk

2 cups ripe peaches peeled and cut into cubes (about 3 peaches)

2 cups fresh blueberries

Vanilla ice cream, for serving

Preheat the oven to 350° F. In a large, deep cast-iron skillet, melt the butter in the preheated oven. Meanwhile, in a bowl, mix the flour, sugar and baking powder. Add the milk and whisk the mixture until just combined. Remove the skillet from the oven, pour the batter into the pan and spread the fruit over the top. Return the skillet to the oven and bake until the batter is cooked through, about 45 minutes.

Serve immediately with ice cream.

If we had to settle on just one life mission, it would be to fight the perception that making cocktails is too difficult to do on a regular basis. We think that the best cocktails—the ones that we want to make and drink all the time—are also the simplest, requiring just a few key ingredients. We're all for opening some bottles of wine at a dinner party or having a case of cold beer at a barbecue, but a few choice cocktails can make your gathering extra special.

This collection of recipes largely features drinks that we've created over the years, from our party days in college to our Saturday night get-togethers in Brooklyn. We've also included some lesser-known classics that we love and think are due for a major resurgence. The recipes start light and bright, with lower-ABV (alcohol by volume) cocktails that are perfect before dinner and on hot summer days, and build up to darker, boozier drinks with serious late-night or winter-warmer potential. Per our cooking style, we like cocktail making to be fun and interactive for our guests; some of our best recipes have been born from mid-party experimentation. Most of these recipes serve one, but all are scalable and easy to make in larger batches. Plus, there's a section of large-format drinks to be made for groups (no special occasion required).

UPSTATE OF MIND

Here's an ingredients list that might seem unexpected, but this combination of bourbon, sparkling wine, ice wine and orange zest creates an effervescent and, dare we say, beguiling cocktail that will keep you coming back for more. The ice wine serves as the sweetener and adds richness to the drink, which is excellent as a pre-dinner aperitif but is versatile enough to keep drinking through the evening.

MAKES 1 COCKTAIL

½ ounce bourbon

¾ ounce Riesling ice wine (or a similar dessert wine)

4 ounces sparkling wine (preferably cava)

1 orange twist, for garnish

In a chilled coupe, swirl the bourbon to coat the inside of the glass, letting any extra remain at the bottom. Add the ice wine to the coupe and top with the sparkling wine. Garnish with the orange peel and serve.

A GREAT MISTAKE

The story of the Negroni Sbagliato cocktail (literally, a "messed up Negroni") goes like this: an apprentice at a bar in Milan mistakenly placed a bottle of Prosecco where the gin was supposed to go. A busy bartender accidentally grabbed the Prosecco and, in a rush, added it to a Negroni instead of gin. The result? A pleasantly bitter cocktail that's perfect for the Italian tradition of late-afternoon *aperitivos*. Sometimes things happen for a (delicious) reason.

NEGRONI SBAGLIATO

We often mix up this classic *aperitivo* to pair with small plates of food ahead of a good meal. With bitter Campari, herbaceous sweet vermouth and citrusy Prosecco, this cocktail whets your appetite and keeps you coming back for another sip.

MAKES 1 COCKTAIL

1½ ounces Campari

1½ ounces sweet vermouth

1½ ounces Prosecco

1 orange twist, for garnish

In a rocks glass filled with ice cubes, combine the Campari and vermouth and stir for 5 seconds. Top with the Prosecco and garnish with the orange twist. Serve immediately.

MAPLE-ROASTED NUTS
WITH MIXED HERBS

This is a great snack to put out at the start of a casual gathering. A mix of nuts is candied with maple syrup and fall-friendly herbs, with delicious salty-sweet results. Be sure to make these at least 90 minutes ahead and let them cool before serving, so they become nicely crunchy.

MAKES 4 SERVINGS

3 tablespoons unsalted butter, melted

¼ cup maple syrup

1 pinch of cayenne pepper

2 cups mixed nuts (pecans, walnuts, almonds or whichever other nuts you like)

Flaky sea salt and freshly ground black pepper

1 teaspoon finely chopped thyme

1 teaspoon finely chopped rosemary

1 teaspoon finely chopped sage

Preheat the oven to 325°F. In a medium bowl, combine the melted butter, maple syrup and cayenne pepper and stir. Add the mixed nuts and toss. On a baking sheet lined with parchment paper, spread the nuts evenly. Bake for 20 minutes or until most of the liquid has evaporated. Remove from the oven, season with salt and pepper and sprinkle evenly with the herbs, stirring to coat. Let the nuts cool for at least 1 hour, then serve.

BURRATA WITH CARAMELIZED SQUASH, PINE NUTS AND GOLDEN RAISINS

Burrata is essentially your favorite fresh mozzarella with a cream-filled center—basically the best thing ever created. As with fresh mozz, burrata classically is partnered with summer's fresh tomatoes and basil. But we see no reason to give up our burrata fix in fall; after tomato season ends, we pair the cheese with sweet roasted squash, pine nuts and golden raisins.

MAKES 4 SERVINGS

2 cups of butternut squash, cut into ¼-inch cubes

¼ cup fresh sage leaves

Olive oil

Flaky sea salt and freshly ground black pepper

1 teaspoon sherry vinegar

2 large balls of burrata

¼ cup pine nuts, lightly toasted

1 tablespoon golden raisins

Sliced and toasted crusty bread

Preheat the oven to 425° F. In a large bowl, toss the squash with the sage, olive oil to coat and salt and pepper. Spread the squash evenly on an oiled rimmed baking sheet. Roast for 20 minutes, without stirring, then stir and roast for 10 minutes longer (or until the squash is well caramelized). When the squash is tender, remove it from the oven and sprinkle with the sherry vinegar.

To serve, plate the burrata on a serving board or platter. Surround the edges of the cheese with the squash, pine nuts and golden raisins. Drizzle the cheese and squash with olive oil and season with salt and pepper. Serve immediately with the bread on the side for spreading the cheese and garnishes.

SPICED HARD CIDER

Cider has had a well-deserved comeback recently, and these days local producers are upping the cider game by making complex, refreshing versions that showcase local fruit (and are much less sweet than former "boozy apple juice" versions). As good as hard cider is drunk straight, we've found that it also makes for a consistently excellent cocktail ingredient. We like to punch up bottled cider by spiking it with applejack, a brandy distilled from apples, and warming spices. We build this drink in a cocktail shaker, infusing the applejack with the spices before topping it with refreshing hard cider.

MAKES 1 COCKTAIL

½ ounce fresh lemon juice

½ ounce simple syrup

1 pinch each ground allspice, cinnamon and cloves

1½ ounces applejack

5 ounces hard cider

Apple slices, for garnish

1 cinnamon stick, for garnish

In a cocktail shaker, combine the lemon juice, simple syrup and spices. Add the applejack and fill the shaker with ice; cap and shake for 5 seconds. Strain into a collins glass filled with ice cubes and top with the hard cider. Garnish with apple slices and cinnamon stick and serve.

THE CAMPFIRE SOUR

This cocktail has a story that, you guessed it, starts with a campfire. A few years back, we were camping in the Adirondacks with a group of friends. The sun went down, a campfire was lit, and a Mason jar of whiskey began making the rounds. Many sips and stories later, we turned in, only to wake up feeling a little oppressed by the morning sun. So we did what any hardy outdoorsman would do: took a sip of the dog that had bitten us the night before. And wouldn't you know, the whiskey tasted amazing. The smoke from the campfire had infused the spirit while the jar sat open, making it smoky, earthy and even better than we'd remembered. We knew right then that we had to recreate that flavor, which brings us to the Campfire Sour. It transports us back to that camping trip, even when we're deep in the urban jungle of New York. We've come up with a method for infusing whiskey without the campfire, but we highly recommend taking a camping trip of your own for smoky-whiskey purposes.

MAKES 1 COCKTAIL

2¼ ounces rye whiskey

1 ounce fresh lemon juice

½ ounce dark maple syrup

One 6-inch rosemary sprig, plus 1 sprig for garnish

In a cocktail shaker, combine the rye, lemon juice and maple syrup. Light the sprig of rosemary on fire and add to the shaker still lit. Cap the shaker and let stand for 30 seconds so that the mixture can infuse with smoke. Fill the shaker with ice; cap and shake for 15 seconds. Strain into a rocks glass containing large ice cubes. Garnish with the remaining rosemary sprig and serve.

FROZEN DRINKS

Step away from the fishbowl-size frozen beverage: anything that comes in a martini glass the size of your head is a bad, hangover-guaranteed idea. But a good frozen cocktail is a thing of summertime beauty that, we're thankful to see, is making appearances at some of our favorite bars year-round. The next three drinks are our top frozen cocktails, but try your own combinations of booze and juice. You can translate most cocktails into frozen versions by making them more concentrated and then blending them with ice to dilute (versus shaking or stirring them). Each of these recipes makes two cocktails (because blenders do better with more volume), which is all the more reason to have a friend join you to test these out.

SPICY MEZCALITA

A mezcalita is a margarita that uses mezcal in addition to tequila; we think it's even better than the classic. Mezcal's smokiness mingles with lime wonderfully, particularly in this frozen version, which is spiced with fresh jalapeño. A salty rim is optional but highly recommended.

MAKES 2 COCKTAILS

3 ounces tequila

1½ ounces mezcal

2 ounces Cointreau

2 ounces fresh lime juice

2 slices fresh jalapeño, plus 2 slices for garnish

2 lime wheels, for garnish

In a blender, combine the tequila, mezcal, Cointreau, lime juice and jalapeño slices. Fill with ice and blend on high until smooth. Pour into rocks glasses and serve, garnished with the remaining jalapeño and lime wheel.

PIÑA COLADA

Forget everything you think you know about piña coladas (at least if your mind immediately goes to syrupy-sweet, premade mixtures loaded with sugar and sadness). This version—the ultimate balance of sweet, boozy, creamy and tart—is the creation of Josh's wife, Rebecca, who makes these piña coladas by the gallon on summer weekend afternoons at the beach. We love her addition of banana, which makes the finished cocktail extra smooth.

MAKES 2 COCKTAILS

6 ounces white rum

6 ounces pineapple juice

6 ounces coconut cream

½ of a banana

1½ ounces fresh lime juice, plus ½ ounce to finish

1 ounce dark rum, to finish

2 lime wheels, for garnish

In a blender, combine the white rum, pineapple juice, coconut cream, banana and 1½ ounces lime juice. Fill with ice and blend on high until smooth. Pour into frosted glasses and finish with the remaining lime juice and dark rum (they'll float on top of the creamy, frozen mixture). Garnish with lime wheels and serve immediately.

FRO-GRONI

Negronis—a boozy blend of gin, Campari and sweet vermouth—have become one of our favorite classic drinks. But when summer rolls around, the all-alcohol mixture becomes too heavy for the hot days, so we end up concocting a slushy, frozen version. Feeling celebratory? Top your glass with a pour of Prosecco post blending.

MAKES 2 COCKTAILS

3 ounces gin

3 ounces Campari

3 ounces sweet vermouth

3 ounces fresh orange juice

2 half wheels of orange, for garnish

Prosecco, for topping (optional)

In a blender, combine the gin, Campari, vermouth and orange juice. Fill with ice and blend on high until smooth. Pour into frosted rocks glasses, garnish with orange wheels and, if you'd like, a pour of Prosecco. Serve immediately.

EL CORONEL

This drink recipe was inspired by a mind-blowing cocktail we had at Trick Dog, our favorite bar in San Francisco. That cocktail used an ingredient that was completely unexpected: mustard! We started playing around with mustard in cocktails and loved the spicy notes it added to a variety of drinks. Here the mustard adds a kick to smoky mezcal, sweet honey and fresh apple cider. Don't worry: we'll let you know if any future ketchup-related experiments are successful too.

MAKES 1 COCKTAIL

2¼ ounces mezcal

¾ ounce fresh lime juice

1½ ounces fresh apple cider

1 teaspoon English mustard powder

1 ounce honey

1 lime wheel, for garnish

In a cocktail shaker, combine the mezcal, lime juice, cider, mustard powder and honey. Stir until the honey and mustard powder dissolve. Fill with ice; cap and shake for 15 seconds. Strain into a rocks glass containing large ice cubes, garnish with the lime wheel and serve.

OLD-FASHIONEDS

We think we officially became adults when we started drinking old-fashioneds — or at least we became adult drinkers who had graduated from drinks that masked the flavor of alcohol to cocktails that celebrated it. An old-fashioned is the purest way to enjoy a spirit, short of drinking it straight: All that goes into it is a spirit, a sweetener and bitters. And when the drink is made correctly, the sugar-bitters elements simply round out and enhance the flavor of the alcohol, instead of distracting from it.

The classic old-fashioned is made with whiskey, sugar and Angostura bitters. But we've found that we can tweak each of these elements to create similarly excellent cocktails. Two things we don't change: (1) we always stir our old-fashioneds, to maintain the drink's clarity and preserve the alcohol's integrity (nothing's worse than a spirit that has had its integrity compromised); and (2) we always serve our old-fashioneds over a single large ice cube. An extra-large cube melts slower than smaller ice cubes, and as the ice melts, the cold water slowly opens up new, subtle flavors in the alcohol.

BARREL-AGED GIN OLD-FASHIONED

Barrel-aged gin is a beautiful thing: the rich, smoky flavors from charred oak barrels round out the gin's sharp, spicy botanical notes. It makes for a brighter, sharper base than whiskey, perfect for a new take on the old-fashioned. Instead of sugar and aromatic bitters, we use honey syrup and citrus bitters in this recipe. If you can't make (or buy) your own barrel-aged gin, añejo tequila is a good substitute. The overall flavor of the drink will be different, but tequila has a similarly spicy, herbaceous quality and it pairs nicely with the honey and citrus.

MAKES 1 COCKTAIL

FOR THE HONEY SYRUP

1 part honey

1 part water

FOR THE COCKTAIL

¾ ounce honey syrup

3 ounces barrel-aged gin (page 199 has more information on making your own barrel-aged gin)

3 dashes citrus bitters
(we like grapefruit bitters)

1 strip grapefruit zest, for garnish

MAKE THE HONEY SYRUP

In a large bowl, combine one part honey and one part water. Whisk together until combined and refrigerate until ready to use.

MAKE THE COCKTAIL

In a mixing glass, combine ¾ ounce of the honey syrup, the gin and the citrus bitters. Add ice and stir for 15 seconds. Strain into a rocks glass containing one extra-large ice cube. Squeeze the grapefruit strip over the cocktail, then add it as a garnish. Serve immediately.

MAPLE BOURBON OLD-FASHIONED

We often use maple syrup in place of regular sugar to sweeten cocktails. Maple syrup is super easy to mix with (it's basically simple syrup with extra flavor), and using a dark variety adds a rich, woodsy taste that goes wonderfully with aged spirits—in this case bourbon.

MAKES 1 COCKTAIL

3 ounces bourbon

¼ ounce maple syrup (preferably dark)

8 dashes aromatic bitters

1 strip of orange zest, for garnish

In a mixing glass, combine the bourbon, maple syrup and bitters. Add ice and stir for 15 seconds. Strain the drink into a rocks glass containing one extra-large ice cube. Squeeze the orange zest over the cocktail, then add it as a garnish. Serve immediately.

CALVADOS OLD-FASHIONED

Calvados, or French apple brandy, is a wonderful base for an apple-scented old-fashioned. Go for a medium-range Calvados (nothing too expensive; the best Calvados should be enjoyed straight up) and mix it with raw sugar and spiced bitters for a cold weather–appropriate cocktail.

MAKES 1 COCKTAIL

2 cubes turbinado sugar

8 dashes aromatic bitters

3 ounces Calvados

1 slice apple, for garnish

1 cinnamon stick, for garnish

In a mixing glass, muddle the sugar cubes with the bitters and a splash of water until the sugar dissolves slightly. Add the Calvados and continue muddling until the sugar is almost entirely dissolved. Add ice and stir for 10 seconds. Strain the drink into a rocks glass containing one extra-large ice cube. Garnish with the apple and a flamed cinnamon stick (light a match and hold the stick up to the flame until it just starts to smolder and smoke). Serve immediately.

JALAPEÑO-AVOCADO MARGARITA

It's easy to equate avocados with guacamole, but the fruit (yes, avocado is a fruit) perfectly lends itself to our spicy take on the classic margarita. This guaca-marg hybrid is proof that avocados aren't just for chip-dipping and taco-topping. By muddling fresh avocado before shaking the cocktail over ice, you create a smooth, creamy base that can be spiked with punchy tequila, tart lime juice and spicy jalapeños. You may want some tortilla chips to snack on with this drink.

MAKES 1 COCKTAIL

1 slice extra-ripe avocado, about ½ inch thick

1 slice fresh jalapeño, plus 1 slice for garnish, seeds removed

1 cilantro sprig, plus 1 sprig for garnish

2¼ ounces blanco tequila

1 ounce Cointreau

1 ounce fresh lime juice

In a cocktail shaker, muddle the avocado, jalapeño and cilantro until the avocado is thoroughly mashed. Add the tequila, Cointreau and lime juice. Add ice, cap and shake vigorously for 20 seconds. Using a fine-mesh strainer, strain into a rocks glass filled with ice. Garnish with the remaining cilantro and jalapeño and serve.

BARREL-AGING

Barrel-aging used to take place only in the dark corners of craft distilleries, but in recent years bartenders have begun to barrel-age their own ingredients, and even finished drinks, in cocktail bars across the country. The process can lend a deep, smoky-sweet undertone to both spirits and cocktails, rounding out the sharp edges of the alcohol.

We've taken barrel-aging out of the distillery and cocktail bar and brought it into the home. And since barrels of any size don't tend to fit in our tiny apartments, we use barrel-aging staves instead. Barrel-aging staves are pieces of charred barrel–grade oak that have been drilled to create maximum surface area and then charred, as the inside of a barrel would be. These staves allow you to rapidly age spirits and cocktails right in a bottle, no barrel required.

Seven to ten days ahead of a party or dinner, we will concoct a cocktail (avoiding fresh juice, as that will spoil) or pick a favorite spirit and drop in a few barrel-aging staves; by the time our friends come around, we have the makings of a unique, custom-aged cocktail.

BARREL-AGED NEGRONI

MAKES 30 OUNCES

10 ounces gin

10 ounces Campari

10 ounces sweet vermouth

2 barrel-aging staves

Orange zest strips, for garnish

In a 32-ounce Mason jar, combine the gin, Campari and vermouth. Add 2 barrel-aging staves. Cap and let the drink age in a cool, dark place for 10 days.

Using a cheesecloth, strain the Negroni into a clean jar or bottle and store in the refrigerator until ready to use. The drink will keep, refrigerated, for up to 2 weeks.

To serve, stir 4 ounces of the barrel-aged Negroni with ice for 10 seconds, strain into a rocks glass filled with ice and garnish with a strip of orange zest. Serve immediately.

BARREL-AGED GIN

MAKES 750 MILLILITERS

One 750-milliliter bottle gin

2 barrel-aging staves

Add 2 barrel-aging staves to the bottle of gin. Cap and let it age for 10 days at room temperature.

Using a cheesecloth, strain the gin into a clean jar or bottle and store in a cool, dark place.

BARREL-AGED MANHATTAN

MAKES 30 OUNCES

20 ounces rye whiskey

10 ounces sweet vermouth

20 dashes aromatic bitters

2 barrel-aging staves

Cocktail cherries, for garnish

In a 32-ounce Mason jar, combine the rye, vermouth and bitters. Add 2 barrel-aging staves. Cap and let the drink age in a cool, dark place for 10 days.

Using a cheesecloth, strain the Manhattan into a clean jar or bottle and store in the refrigerator until ready to use. The drink will keep, refrigerated, for up to 2 weeks.

To serve, stir 4 ounces of the barrel-aged Manhattan with ice for 10 seconds, strain into a chilled rocks glass or coupe and garnish with cherries. Serve immediately.

THE BOULEVARDIER

Much as we love creating cocktail recipes, we also love classic drinks with a story. The Boulevardier is one of those. A darker, more sultry Negroni in which bourbon is substituted for gin, this drink was invented in the late 1920s by an American in Paris who ran an expat magazine also called (you guessed it) *The Boulevardier*. As with all lore involving cocktails, you have to take that story with a grain of salt (or a dash of bitters). At any rate, bourbon, Campari and vermouth play well together, and the drink is refreshing enough to be a great choice year-round.

MAKES 1 COCKTAIL

1½ ounces bourbon

1 ounce Campari

1 ounce sweet vermouth

1 strip orange zest, for garnish

In a mixing glass, combine the bourbon, Campari and vermouth. Add ice and stir for 30 seconds. Strain into a chilled rocks glass containing one large ice cube. Squeeze the orange zest over the cocktail, drop it into the drink and serve.

LARGE-FORMAT COCKTAILS

Although all our cocktail recipes can be scaled up for party-throwing purposes, we're huge fans of large-format drinks dedicated to serving a crowd—e.g., punch. A far cry from the Jungle Juice trash-can concoctions of our college days, these cocktails are flavorful drinks featuring fresh ingredients and high-quality spirits. They are incredibly easy to make, which means they're perfect for big get-togethers. Just stock up on a handful of basic ingredients and, whenever drinks run low, you can quickly throw together another batch.

PLANTER'S PUNCH

One of the most iconic rum punches around, Planter's Punch is said to have originated in Charleston, South Carolina, with inspiration from Jamaica. Of course, that's often disputed (#drunkhistory). Suffice to say, it's made with hot, steamy climates in mind and is meant to be a bracing cooldown. Planter's Punch always includes dark rum, fruit juice and grenadine. We keep the flavors clean by sticking to simple citrus juices and buying only high-quality craft grenadine. This punch is an easy fit for any kind of gathering, but we like it just as much in winter when we're craving a reminder of summer heat.

MAKES 10 COCKTAILS

One 750-milliliter bottle aged rum

5 ounces grenadine

3 ounces simple syrup

5 ounces fresh lemon juice

12 ounces fresh lime juice

Wheels of mixed citrus (lemon, lime and/or orange), for garnish

Aromatic bitters, to finish

In a large punch bowl or carafe, combine the rum, grenadine, simple syrup and lemon and lime juices. Add ice until it's level with the liquid and stir to combine. Garnish with the citrus wheels and 10 hefty dashes of the bitters over the surface of the punch. Serve immediately.

BURNT-SATSUMA CHAMPAGNE PUNCH

We first served this punch for a New Year's Eve party a few years back and have since made it part of our year-round cocktail rotation. The drink has a unique undertone of citrus and smoke, which comes from orange slices that we caramelize under the broiler. Then we build a classic Champagne cocktail, using simple syrup, bitters and good Champagne, and add a kick of vodka. We love to use satsuma oranges, a flavorful member of the mandarin family, when they're in season, but any oranges will do.

MAKES 10 COCKTAILS

Ten ¼-inch thick slices of satsuma oranges (or other oranges, if unavailable)

5 ounces simple syrup

15 dashes orange bitters

5 ounces vodka

One 750-milliliter bottle Champagne, chilled

4 strips satsuma orange zest, for garnish

On a baking sheet lined with foil, broil the satsuma orange slices under high heat until slightly charred, about 5 minutes. Let cool.

In a large carafe or punch bowl, combine the simple syrup, orange bitters, vodka and charred orange slices with enough ice to fill the carafe or bowl halfway. Stir for 5 seconds. Add the Champagne, stirring once to combine.

To serve, pour the punch into chilled coupes and garnish with the orange zest, Serve immediately.

ROSÉ NOIR

Everyone's all "rosé all day!" these days. We're all for it, especially when we can combine sparkling rosé with blackberry preserves and craft vodka. Loaded with sweet Meyer lemons, this punch is great for a casual brunch party but special enough for a celebratory dinner. This recipe can easily be doubled (or tripled) to satisfy a larger crowd too.

MAKES 10 COCKTAILS

15 ounces vodka

8 tablespoons blackberry preserves

4 ounces fresh Meyer lemon juice

One 750-milliliter bottle sparkling rosé, chilled

1 handful fresh blackberries, for garnish

10 Meyer lemon wheels, for garnish

In a large punch bowl or carafe, combine the vodka, preserves and Meyer lemon juice with enough ice to fill the bowl or carafe halfway. Stir for 5 seconds. Add the sparkling rosé and stir once. Garnish with the fresh blackberries and Meyer lemon wheels. Serve in coupes or Champagne glasses and garnished with lemon twists.

winter

GATHERING

It can be tempting to hibernate when winter turns especially cold in Brooklyn. Our apartments, so warm! Outside, so chilly! And though we occasionally give in to the inclination to hunker down with delivery food and a six-pack on a snowy Sunday, other times we like to motivate our friends to bundle up and come over for brunch. Getting together when the weather is less agreeable can make these gatherings a little more special: What's a better definition of friendship than trekking through snow and sleet to hang out?

Regardless of the effort involved, Sunday brunch is a great way to get people together. There's nothing like cozying up around platters of fresh biscuits with country ham, creamy eggs with sharp cheddar and spicy greens, and bracing mugs of hot buttered rum. We especially love it when brunch goes on all day, maybe even stretching into a casual dinner party (or an even more casual delivery–with–some–six–packs hangout).

BUTTERMILK BISCUITS WITH HONEY BUTTER AND COUNTRY HAM

We love these homemade buttermilk biscuits, made from a family recipe that's been passed down over the generations. They're flaky, light and savory, with plenty of buttery richness. Shortening is a must here to get the right texture, though chilled lard will do just fine. Good luck eating just one of these babies, especially when you pair them with sweet honey butter and paper-thin slices of salty country ham.

MAKES 15 TO 20 SMALL BISCUITS

2 cups all-purpose flour

2 heaping teaspoons baking powder

1 teaspoon fine salt

4 heaping tablespoons solid shortening, chilled

1 cup buttermilk, well shaken

4 tablespoons unsalted butter, softened

¼ cup honey

12 very thin slices country ham, for serving

Preheat the oven to 475° F. In a large bowl, sift together the flour, baking powder and salt. Using a pastry cutter, blend in the shortening until the mixture looks grainy, like fine cornmeal. Add the buttermilk and stir with a fork until the dough just holds together (you can add more buttermilk if the dough is too dry).

Shape the dough into a ball and turn it out onto a floured surface. Using a rolling pin, roll out the dough about ¼ inch thick. Using a 2-inch biscuit cutter, cut out 15 to 20 rounds. Bake the biscuits on an unlined baking sheet for 8 to 10 minutes or until the tops just turn golden brown.

Meanwhile, in a medium bowl, combine the softened butter and honey and stir. When the biscuits are done, transfer them to a serving board or platter; serve alongside the honey butter and ham slices for guests to create their own ham biscuits.

WINTER CITRUS SALAD
WITH FRESH MINT AND LIME

Winter is prime time for fresh oranges, grapefruits and other citrus, and we make full use of the seasonal crop with this simple and refreshing sliced-fruit salad. A squeeze of fresh lime perks up all the flavors of the mixed citrus, and fresh mint finishes off the dish.

MAKES 6 SERVINGS

1 large grapefruit, chilled

1 large orange, chilled

2 small blood oranges, chilled

1 lime

Fresh mint leaves, for garnish

Peel the grapefruit, orange and blood orange with a paring knife, being sure to remove any white pith.

Slice the citrus into rounds and arrange on a platter. Squeeze the lime over the citrus and sprinkle with fresh mint leaves. Serve immediately.

SLOW-COOKED EGGS WITH AGED CHEDDAR AND SPICY GREENS

This recipe is all about patience, but these cheesy eggs are worth the wait. The slower you cook them, the creamier the texture becomes. It is Sunday, after all—what's the rush? Seek out an aged cheddar for this dish; the sharp saltiness is perfect with the creamy, rich eggs and peppery greens.

MAKES 4 TO 6 SERVINGS

12 large eggs

Flaky sea salt and freshly ground black pepper

1 tablespoon olive oil

½ cup grated aged cheddar

2 cups spicy greens (like arugula or mizuna)

2 tablespoons finely chopped chives, for garnish

In a large mixing bowl, crack the eggs and whisk them together with a pinch of salt and pepper. In a large skillet, heat the oil over low heat. Add the eggs and cook, stirring constantly, until they start to thicken, about 15 minutes (they should still look runny). Add the grated cheese and greens and continue to cook, stirring, until the eggs are cooked through but still soft, about 5 minutes more. Remove the skillet from the heat; transfer the eggs to a serving platter or bowl and garnish with the chives. Serve immediately.

MAPLE HOT-BUTTERED RUM

Most of us have heard of hot buttered rum, but not many know what it is, or if it really has butter in it (it does). Hot-buttered rum is as warming, rich and delicious as it sounds; even better, it's simple to make. Some versions use honey or brown sugar as the sweetener, but we like dark maple syrup, which adds real depth of flavor.

MAKES 1 COCKTAIL

1½ ounces aged rum

¾ ounce dark maple syrup

1 teaspoon unsalted butter

1 pinch of freshly grated cinnamon

Boiling water

Freshly grated nutmeg

1 cinnamon stick, for garnish

In a mug, combine the rum, maple syrup, butter and cinnamon. Top off with boiling water, stirring to incorporate the ingredients and melt the butter. Garnish with the nutmeg and cinnamon stick and serve.

THANK YOU!

ERIC

Over the past several years, the list of people whom I want to thank continues to grow. Many thanks to my family, which has always encouraged me, especially my mom, the most creative person that I know — you taught me to bring people together and encouraged my creativity, and I couldn't ask for more. To our friends and co-workers: You are the best hand models, taste testers, sounding boards and contributors to our (sometimes harebrained) ideas. To my wife, Bianca: Thank you for everything. Without a doubt, you are the most welcoming and loving person I know, and have served as an inspiration in all things. I look forward to a lifetime of dinners, parties and fun with you. Thank you for everything. Josh: I've heard that if you love what you do for work, you will never work another day in your life. Thanks for making this a reality; I'm looking forward to continuing the adventure.

JOSH

To my parents, thank you for instilling in me a passion for all things food and drink, for teaching me what it means to truly welcome someone into your home and for funding my obscenely expensive cookbook-buying habit for so many years. Thank you for encouraging me to travel, find my own path and believe anything is achievable. To Eric, thanks for being the best business partner and friend I could ever hope for - I'm pretty pumped for everything to come. To our friends who gave their time, advice, apartments and support to make this book a reality: thank you times a million. Last, and most importantly, to Rebecca: Thank you for being my inspiration, sounding board and tremendously patient better half. I am so lucky to have you as my co-host for the lifetime of parties ahead of us.

ERIC + JOSH

A big thank you to Lauren for diving into our madness head-first and helping to create an amazing body of writing. You are seriously awesome. Thank you to Marylou for lending us your addicting cobbler recipe. Thank you to Tay Tay for passing down the tradition of delicious buttermilk biscuits. Thanks to the whole team that supported the creation of this book: Jordan, Justin, Jessica, Elizabeth, Tyler, Ryan E., Chris, Nick, Lucas, Amie, Nicole, Ryan K., Evan and Carlo (also: Stanley and Maplethorpe, obviously). Last, but definitely not least, A huge thanks to Scott for visually documenting 10 years of our culinary lives (i.e. our entire lives) in one book of simple recipes.

ABOUT THE AUTHORS

Eric Prum and Josh Williams have been best friends since they met on their first day of college at the University of Virginia. Today, they are business partners in W&P Design, the company they co-founded in Brooklyn, New York, in 2012.

W&P Design applies innovative design to the food and beverage world, with the simple mission of helping you eat and drink better (while having fun doing it). Since founding W&P Design, Eric and Josh have created more than 200 food and beverage products, including tools, kits and print and digital content. Among their most popular creations are the Mason Shaker, a Mason jar cocktail shaker; the Carry On Cocktail Kit, which contains the tools and ingredients to mix craft cocktails mid-flight; and the Peak Ice product line, a collection of innovative tools for making ice in your home freezer.

W&P Design's products and recipes have been featured in The New York Times, Food & Wine and Bon Appétit, among many other publications.

Eric and Josh are also the authors of *Shake: A New Perspective on Cocktails* and *Infuse: Oil, Spirit, Water*.

INDEX

DOVETAIL

Published by Dovetail Press in Brooklyn, New York, a division of Assembly Brands LLC.

For details or ordering information, contact the publisher at the address below
or email **info@dovetail.press**.

Dovetail Press
42 West Street #403
Brooklyn, NY 11222
www.dovetail.press

Library of Congress Cataloging-in-Publication data is on file with the publisher.

ISBN: 978-0-9898882-1-9

First Edition

Printed in China

10 9 8 7 6 5 4 3 2 1

For more recipes and to purchase the tools used in *Host*, visit **www.wandpdesign.com**